Prepper's Pantry

A Food Survival Guide

By Robert Paine

© 2013

And above all – Enjoy!

Table of Contents

Introduction

Preparing for a sudden economic downturn is something that has gotten a lot of mainstream media attention in the last few years. With the popularity of the television show "Doomsday Preppers," people who were not at all involved in the "prepper" lifestyle are suddenly interested in developing a stockpile of necessities for that "just in case" day that preppers talk about.

What is a "prepper"? Simply put, it's one who prepares for the possibility that the world may catastrophically change at some point in our future, leaving food supplies, fuel supplies, and our current lifestyles drastically changed. Those reasons for change could be local, regional, or even on a worldwide scale.

Before the availability of long distance trucking, and even international shipping, of fresh meats and produce, most people "prepped," to some degree. Most likely, your grandparents had a garden, and canned or otherwise preserved the food they grew and harvested throughout the summer, so that they would have food for the coming winter. They may have even had a cow and a pig or two, and butchered regularly, either freezing or canning the meat to add to their winter stores. If you read the "Little House On The Prairie" books when you were younger, you were introduced to the prepper lifestyle; in those days, preparing for the winter was a matter of necessity. Without the proper supplies in place, families would die of starvation.

Modern supermarkets have made the need to do this kind of yearly prepping all but disappear. Almost any type of fruit or vegetable is available year round, if you're willing to either pay a high enough price for it, or buy it already canned or frozen. Modern meat packing plants butcher cows and pigs daily, with the animals being brought to feedlots a few weeks before slaughter, to pack on pounds and insure that you can buy bacon whenever you're in the mood for it. Modern food preservation methods mean that food can sit on store and home shelves for months, even years, without going bad. Truthfully, it's easier, and often cheaper, to buy your produce already canned, than it is to grow a garden and preserve it yourself. So much easier, in fact, that home food preservation is rapidly becoming a lost art.

Many people with the prepper mindset have developed a balance between preserving fresh food at home, and the use of supermarkets or wholesale clubs to enhance their personal stores. The methods of preparing that work best for you will depend on many factors such as your budget, the availability of certain tools and kitchen appliances, space, and your personal reasons for prepping.

Preppers stockpile food for a variety of reasons. Some people, much like our grandparents, stockpile food because their work is seasonal. Maybe the primary wage earner is a construction worker, who doesn't work much in the winter. Some people prepare because they are contract employees, and they know that they may not have a contract at any given point. Having three or six months' worth of food on hand is one less expense they will have to worry about while job hunting. They may be preparing for an economic downturn, or simply taking advantage of sale prices. Finally, they may be preparing for TEOTWAWKI, or The End Of The World As We Know It.

The TEOTWAWKI scenario is one that has been gaining ground in recent years. There are many reasons people think that humanity will undergo a catastrophic change in the coming years. Peak oil, the theory that we have drilled the most oil we will ever get, and that available supplies will slowly dwindle to extinction, is an often-cited fear. Climate change or catastrophic weather event are also near the top of the list of reasons why people prep. There are people afraid of a shadow government or New World Order, and there are some people concerned about a biblical Armageddon.

The reasons why you prep really don't matter. What matters is how long you're prepping for, and the means you go about doing it. This guide will show you how to determine your food needs, no matter how long you will be prepping for, and will discuss various methods of obtaining and storing food stockpiles.

Chapter One: Determining Your Food Preparation Needs

Determining your food preparation needs can be dependent upon many factors. The two most important factors are length of time you're preparing for, and how many people you will need to feed with the food that you stockpile. People prepping for seasonal job loss may be prepping for three or six months. A "Doomsday Prepper" may be prepping for years.

Another major determining factor in building your food stockpile is space. You need to determine if you've got enough protected storage space for the food that you want and need to store. This storage space can be inside your house, in your garage, or in secure outbuildings. Make sure you can protect your food storage from animals of all types, and from wet, freezing, or humid conditions. Below are different suggestions for storage

Glass – Ideal for most foods, glass can take the form of jars of water bath or pressure canned foods, vacuum-sealed storage containers, or containers with screwed on lids. Glass also works very well for freezing soups, broths, and foods not appropriate for canning, if you have the space in your freezer. Cost can be considerable. A water bath canner can run you $40-$60, and canning jars can cost up to $10/dozen if bought new. The explosion in popularity of Mason jar crafts has made it difficult to find used canning jars for a reasonable price. However, if you take careful care of your jars, you won't need to buy many more with subsequent canning seasons. Expect to pay between $100 and $200 for a good quality pressure canner. Glass does a good job of keeping out smaller pests like bugs and mice, but the breakable jars can result in food loss if they are knocked over.

Plastic jars – The great thing about plastic jars is that they can usually be found or scrounged for free. The peanut butter and mayonnaise that you're probably already buying comes in them, and your friends, family and neighbors may be willing to save their own for you. Craigslist or freecycle are also great sources. Plastic jars can hold dehydrated foods as long as you're storing them in dark pantries or cabinets. They're also good for longer-term storage of dried herbs and spices. Generally, you can also use them for freezing, too. Try to find BPA free plastic. The cost here is minimal, since you're mainly going to be using jars you already own. Plastic storage systems can be purchased, but avoid those with square tops, and those that can be purchased at dollar stores, if you want to use them for freezing. Plastic jars will keep out bugs, but not mice. If you only use these jars for freezing, then you will have less overall food loss.

Plastic bags – While these aren't great for long-term storage (unless you're also going to be putting the filled plastic bags into larger hard plastic containers), they are just fine for short-term storage, and the freezer bags are fine for freezing smaller cuts of meat. Just don't thaw in the microwave or reheat inside the bags. Just a few dollars a week will keep you supplied with plastic bags. If you're storing in plastic bags, it's a good idea to rotate your food stock into fresh bags every six months or so. Plastic breaks down over time, giving your food items less protection.

Vacuum bags – Vacuum systems are ideal for long-term storage of many items. They are great for long-term storage of dehydrated foods, and keep any frozen food fresher, for longer. Vacuum storage also works well for matches, first aid kits, and paper goods for your bug out bags, as the vacuum bags will keep them dry while they sit in storage waiting to be used, or if you need to bug out in the rain. A vacuum system can cost up to $200, and the bags aren't very cheap either, but used efficiently, they are definitely worth the financial investment.

Most households will find themselves using a combination of these methods, depending on the types and sources of foods they are stockpiling. In addition to the costs above, if you're thinking of purchasing a dehydrator, you can get a basic one for around $50, at your local discount store or online, while the top of the line Excalibur dehydrator is about $300. If you're going to have a garden and dry your own produce from there, the Excalibur is definitely a better choice. If you are looking to make the best use of sale prices or warehouse club stock-ups, then you can go with a smaller model. Dehydrating and canning are both time consuming, and can be fairly labor intensive, but in terms of ability to preserve the most food, and keeping your own personal costs down while retaining the best quality possible, these are definitely the methods to go for.

Both dehydrating and canning also offer the added bonus of being able to put together "convenience foods." These meals are often cooked in one pot, and cook up fairly quickly, so you don't have to be busy in the kitchen for hours. This is an important consideration if both parents work, or if, during a TEOTWAWKI situation, both adults would need to be engaged in manual labor that would take them out of the kitchen. By the time you come in from what you're doing, you're tired and hungry, and the less you have to wait for food to cook, the better. Dehydrated meals often take less time to reheat, but they are better than nothing.

Now that you've been introduced to basic methods of food preservation, it's time to figure out how to determine your household's needs for a specific time frame. Keeping these methods in mind, you'll need to determine how much storage space that you have. For a family of two, a set of shelves stashed in a corner and a bit of freezer space could easily store three months worth of food. A family of six that wants to stockpile a years' worth of food is going to need much more room.

There is no hard and fast formula for determining how much space your stockpile will take up. That's dependent upon many factors. For example, dehydrated carrots take up much less space than canned carrots. However, if you're storing primarily dehydrated food, you'll need to store more water than the basic recommendations of one gallon per person, per day, or have access to a clean, steady water supply. If you're storing canned carrots, you can use the packaging fluid, which is mostly water, as a base for cooking rice, potatoes, or re-hydrating some other type of dried food.

You also want to make sure that your stockpile contains food that can actually be made into meals. It's great to have several flats of vegetables, cases of pasta and 18 gallons of water. But without some type of sauce or seasoning, you may not be very happy with your food choices. Children certainly wouldn't want to eat the meal you could come up with, with those ingredients.

So as you're building your stockpile, you'll need to actually plan what meals you can make with those ingredients, and how you can best preserve or obtain the foods needed to fill in the holes on your meal plan. If you're doing any of your prepping by buying items on sale at your grocery store, it can be particularly easy to fall into this trap. But if you think creatively and out of the box, you can make more healthy, structured meals that will feed your family.

If you're looking at this week's store sale ad and you notice that green chiles are on sale, then you can buy a bushel of roasted green chiles, and make green chili to be canned. For that you'll need pork, some chicken broth, and perhaps some tomatoes. Well, last week, chicken was on sale, so if you stocked up on that, you have plenty available to put into a pot and make broth with, also yielding you several pounds of cooked chicken for additional meals. Also in this week's sale ad are pork ribs. While ribs aren't the traditional cut that green chili is made with, there's no rule that says you can't use them. That green chili will make an excellent topping for burritos or is great in a bowl by itself.

So here's what you have determined from looking at this week's sale ad:

- Green chiles are on sale, so green chili can be made and canned

- Pork Ribs are on sale, so they can be the meat in the green chili

- Pork Ribs are on sale, so canning some meat from them will yield some very tender pork that could be added to BBQ sauce and served on sandwiches or over mashed potatoes

- Chickens were on sale last week, so chicken broth can be made. The resulting chicken meat can be frozen and used for casseroles or as filling for the burritos that the green chili will smother.

For the burritos, you'll also need to buy beans, and the ingredients to make tortillas (flour, baking soda, lard, salt), and, if you're sure you'll have power to keep your freezer running during whatever event you're stockpiling for, some cheese to go on the burritos. Add some rice and vegetables to the smothered burritos and you've got a great meal.

So with the purchase of a bushel of green chiles and several pounds of pork ribs and chicken, you've already got some key ingredients for several meals. Now that you've made some initial plans, you can sit down and do some planning.

As you're planning your stockpile, the most important factor to keep in mind is food fatigue. Using the scenario above, you could make enough green chili to feed your family for several days. But if you've ever given the side eye to the turkey that's been the mainstay of every meal for the last four days after Thanksgiving, you can understand the issue of food fatigue. This becomes even more critical in TEOTWAWKI situations because people are often performing tasks they are unfamiliar with, and doing more manual labor than they were used to, and every single calorie that is consumed is important, because each calorie is being used, rather than sitting there doing nothing but becoming fat. If you are sick of the food that's being served to you, you won't eat it. Your body won't let you. It's not a matter of convincing yourself that you need to eat. Your body will trigger responses such as nausea that will prevent you from being able to eat the food, and you will go without those much-needed calories. It's extremely important that you plan to have as wide a variety as possible of food available for your family in these extreme situations.

It's a good idea to build your stockpile a week at a time. This way, crucial ingredients aren't lost in the shuffle. You keep your mind on your purpose and can make sure that things are done efficiently. It may take you three or four weeks' worth of shopping to build a week's worth of stockpile, if you are doing most of your stockpiling from the grocery or warehouse store. If you are doing part of your stockpile from a garden or from butchering your own meat, planning this way still gives you a good idea of what you do need to buy at the store, so that you can fill in any holes as certain foods go on sale.

As you can see, just from this week's sale ad, you've got two meals planned, with notes about what you still need to obtain. Because you're familiar with different types of food preservation methods, you can note what methods you want to use for different items. How much of these items to buy and keep stocked, or preserved, will be determined from this list.

It's important to note that by using a list like this, you're giving yourself ideas. Things may happen that prevent you from using the list in its entirety. But a list like this is a starting point-somewhere for you to start making your plans. You can make other tables like the one above for different weeks. Look at how many quarts or pints of green chili you got canned, determine how many you want to keep for non stockpile use, and then go through your stockpile meal plans and add in either smothered burritos or a bowl of green chili every few weeks until you would have gone through the stock that you made.

To fill in the rest of the meal plan, you'll want to determine your garden plans, if you have space and time to garden, and look at the sale ads and determine what would be cheaper to buy at the warehouse store, if you have space. So maybe next week you add a spaghetti dinner, because pasta and sauce are on sale. If you can afford to, buy enough pasta and sauce for several weeks, and fill in those weeks as you need them. Remember that when you bought beans for the burritos, you bought a large bag. You can plan a meal with beans and canned ham, or use beans as a side to a chicken casserole. Try to find and print new recipes to add to the versatility of the foods that you are stockpiling.

Above all, and especially if you have children, buy food that you are familiar with. If your goal is to supplement your food stores with items like rice and beans, that store well for years, make sure that you introduce these foods to your family before they become a necessity. It's great to have 12 quarts of green chili ready to go in an emergency, but if your kids have never eaten it, you may find mealtime to be a battle, and that's one thing you won't have time for if you're in a TEOTWAWKI situation! If you're relying on either home-canned or store bought canned meats to be an important part of your stockpile, make a meal with these once a month or more, so that your family can get used to the texture and flavor of these foods. The same goes with any foods that you are planning on using in a different form than you usually do. Canned spinach tastes vastly different than fresh, which tastes vastly different than frozen.

As you're making your plans, take special note of quantities. If there's only one or two in your household, then you don't need to plan meals that will feed six, unless you're planning on inviting people with marketable skills to join you and create a compound of sorts for a TEOTWAWKI situation. But also remember that you may need more calories in that type of situation. Further, we tend to want to consume more calories in winter than summer, and if you will no longer have access to a gym or somewhere out of the elements to work out, that could be an issue, if you're not the one doing manual labor. Also remember that a pound of dehydrated food does not equal a pound of fresh, and that a pint of soup is pretty close to the condensed soups that you see in the store, but that you won't need to add water.

You should also remember that if you are in a TEOTWAWKI situation, your very survival depends on the quality of the food you are consuming. This is where you need to balance the so very important need to buy food that you are familiar with, and the need to make sure that each calorie you consume is one that your body can use as fuel. In other words, don't plan boxed macaroni and cheese too often, even though your kids love it and it's something you're certain they will eat. Make sure that they are getting plenty of fruits, vegetables, and whole grains now so they are used to it when they are essential. If you're going to be hunting for your meat, make sure everyone in your family knows what venison and wild game tastes like so they aren't surprised when that may be the only protein you have access to. Make whole grain breads part of your meal plans now, so that when you're relying on them to fill hungry bellies, the kids will enjoy their flavor and texture rather than find them new and intimidating.

This is why, what you're preparing for is of huge importance for what you prep. While it should always be a goal to serve the healthiest meals possible, boxed macaroni and cheese is quick and easy for many families and its okay to indulge once in awhile. If you're not preparing for a TEOTWAWKI situation, it may be something that you want to add to your food stockpile when it's on sale. If you're planning for a time when the primary income earner will be seasonally laid off, you need to remember to include that person for lunch, especially if that's something you don't normally do because they are at work.

You also have to decide, especially if you're planning for a large group, just how strict you should be with serving sizes. Nutritional guidelines state that a moderately active 28-year-old woman should have 2,000 calories per day, and a moderately active 28-year-old man should have 2600 calories per day. Your goal should be to make sure as many of those calories as possible come from vegetables, whole grains, and lean proteins, but you must also make the decision as to whether or not you are going to allow extra servings. Is the 28-year-old man extra hungry today because he did more physical labor? Will an extra slice of bread take him over the 2600 calories you planned for him to consume today, and is that going to leave you short of the allotted food for the week or the month? Will you take the time to measure out each serving of food to make sure that each person only gets an exact amount of food? If you're able to, you should try to plan at least 10% more calories, per day, than those guidelines suggest. If you have extras, they can either be consumed as leftovers, fed to farm animals, or used as bait when hunting. Again, there's a fine line between extras and waste, and if you're in a position where you need to stockpile food for any reason, you should plan to avoid waste as often as possible.

If you're stockpiling for a poverty situation, you will probably be able to save leftovers, and should plan to use them for later lunches or as parts of different meals. A beef roast makes great soup or beef stroganoff later in the week. But if you're prepping for a TEOTWAWKI situation, you won't be able to refrigerate those leftovers, and storing them in a root cellar could lead to pest infestation. In that case, you could can the leftovers, over an open fire, or on a woodstove, you could feed a neighbor, or you could use the leftovers for animal feed or bait. When prepping for a TEOTWAWKI situation, you may find it useful to cut meats into smaller portions or can most of it ahead of time to reduce your waste later on.

Chapter Two: How to obtain the food you'll need

Determining what is best to buy, where, is one of the most complex issues when you're prepping for long-term food storage. Supermarket, warehouse clubs, and farmer's markets are great choice for food you can't grow yourself-or grow enough of for long-term preps. Growing your own offers other advantages as well.

Supermarkets offer a few distinct advantages over warehouse stores when it comes to long term food stockpiling: size of the units, store brands, and coupons. When you're looking at canned condensed soup, it's easier to store smaller cans than the larger ones available at the warehouse stores. Something like condensed soup can't be easily repackaged if you can't use the entire container quickly, and it can be difficult to carry a large number ten can through your house if you're weaving around small children and newborn puppies. Store brands often carry a substantial savings per unit, even when compared to warehouse club prices. And coupons are an amazing tool, giving you the ability to stock up on name brand products at rock bottom prices.

Shopping at a supermarket also brings with it a definite set of challenges. First off, you may be limited in what quantities you can buy. Many stores limit quantities to make sure they don't run out of a specific item. On the other side of that coin, a store may be out of an item you want to buy.

Despite the bad side of supermarket shopping, the unit sizes are definitely a plus when it comes to many items, especially if you won't be feeding an army. The supermarket gives you the opportunity to buy in the sizes you need rather than the food service sizes that are often what's available at warehouse clubs. If canned soups, fruits, and vegetables are part of your preparations, it's a good idea to buy them at your supermarket. You can even buy single servings of many of these items, which are ideal if there are just a couple of people in your household, although they are more expensive in the long run.

If your budget is tight, supermarket store brands often offer the best deal in the smaller sizes, on a regular basis. In other words, supermarket store brands don't often go on sale, but when you need something to fill out your stockpile, and you can't wait for it to be on sale, buying the store brand is usually the way to go, especially with the basics like canned soups, tomato products, and fruits. There is usually very little difference in the quality of these canned items when compared to the name brands. Supermarket store brands are also the best way to stock up on baking staples like sugar, flour, cornstarch and salt. While the name brands of these items go on sale, they don't do so very often, and without careful watching and coupon gathering, the store brands are still a better deal.

Of course, coupon shopping is often the best way to get the most bang for your buck. Paired with in store sales, manufacturer's coupons can be a great way to bring down prices on your favorite name brand items, and using them can quickly grow your stockpile. However, coupons take time to clip and organize, and coupon shopping can be frustrating if your item is out of stock or difficult to locate. If you have time, though, by matching coupons with store sales you can see prices that are up to 75% off of the regular price. That's a pretty significant savings, and a great way to build your stockpile.

Fresh produce can also be a good purchase at your supermarket, if several factors fall into place:

- You can't grow the produce yourself

- You can't get the produce locally at a Farmer's Market

- The produce is on sale for cheaper than you could get it at the warehouse club, if you have a membership

-You have the means to preserve the produce

Many fruits and vegetables may meet all of these criteria, depending on where you live. If you can afford to buy organic fruits and vegetables, chances are, you're going to find them for a more reasonable price at the supermarket than at the Farmer's Market, although if you are buying in bulk, you may be able to negotiate for a better price at the Farmer's Market. Organic produce doesn't go on sale as often as non-organic, so if you have the time to process fifty pounds of potatoes or tomatoes, try the Farmer's Market instead of the supermarket. If you're buying at the Farmer's Market, chances are the produce was still on the plant or in the ground twelve hours before you bought it. The same cannot be said of most supermarket produce, even when it's organic and local.

Of course, not everyone can afford to buy organic. It's okay if your food choices can't go that route. By stockpiling, you may find that you're able to switch to buying organic over time. When you're not buying organic, you may find that the supermarket is a great resource for adding fresh produce, that you process at home, to your stockpile.

Walking into a warehouse club for the first time can be an overwhelming experience. Some clubs are larger than entire malls, and within their walls are literally almost everything you'll ever need, from birth to death. From diapers to caskets, you can find, or order, almost anything at a warehouse club.

There are a lot of good buys here, especially if you're shopping for a family or large group. However, when shopping at a warehouse club, you need two things: space to store your stockpile, and the time to repackage a good deal of what you buy.

Produce can be a great deal at warehouse clubs, if you have the ability to preserve what you buy, or you will use it before it goes bad. Prices are often very reasonable, but the produce is rarely local. However, you can get out-of-season produce for a much better price than you can at the supermarket, as long as you are prepared to buy in larger quantities.

Warehouse clubs are also the best place to buy important pantry items like rice, beans, most cooking oils, and coffee. This is also where you want to purchase your stocks of pre-packaged items like granola bars, and breakfast cereals. And because warehouse clubs market to restaurants, this is a great place to stock up on single serving packets of items that would require refrigeration after opening, like mayonnaise. Paper goods, including storage bags, are also often a good deal at warehouse clubs.

In most regions, with good soil and inexpensive water, growing your own fruits and vegetables is by far the least expensive way to stockpile food for the long term. Even if you have limited space, you can use alternate growing methods to improve the quality of food you're able to provide for your family and yourself.

Growing your own food doesn't have to mean selling your home and moving out to the country. Even suburban and urban homes can grow at least some of their food. Container gardening, vertical gardening, and putting chickens in your back yard or apartment rooftop can be viable ways to grow at least some of your own food without having much land to call your own.

Chapter Three: The List - The best methods for obtaining the foods you need to build your stockpile

This list will primarily focus on whole, basic foods. Obviously, if you're including prepared food in your preps, you're buying those at the best price you can find, straight off of store shelves. Determining the best methods for stocking up on whole foods can be a bit more difficult. This list is a guide to help you determine which methods are right for you.

When you're doing your shopping, you need to choose simple, utility type foods. You may have a favorite source for your cinnamon or a favorite variety of heirloom tomato. While these are tasty, in a poverty or TEOTWAWKI situation, you want simple and hardy-and your budget may dictate what you can buy. When choosing your foods and/or seeds, choose varieties that will store well, and that don't need special growing environments or extra attention. You may be doing extra work, and while gardening will have an entirely new meaning when it needs to yield enough food for your family for a year, your time there may still be limited.

The produce aisle – Clearly, growing your own is the best way to go here. However, not everyone has the space, or the time to process the food for long-term storage.

Potatoes - These dehydrate well, and store well through the winter, without processing, in the right conditions. Buy instant potato flakes for mashed potatoes or to bulk up bread recipes, and boxed potatoes for different flavors. Dehydrated potatoes go well in soups and stews.

Onions - These dehydrate well and store well through the winter. They can also be diced and then frozen, but are stringy and limp when thawed so make sure your dices are fairly small. Do not buy pre-frozen.

Lettuces - Most lettuces do not store well. Spinach, diced and frozen, makes a good addition to soups and sauces, but won't be good plain.

Celery - Celery both dehydrates and freezes well.

Carrots - Dehydrate, can or freeze. If you can't grow your own, you'll get the most bang for your buck by buying canned.

Green Beans - Freeze or can. If you can't grow your own, buy canned.

Yams or sweet potatoes - DO NOT CAN. Your best bet here is to buy canned.

Corn - Freeze, can, or dehydrate. If you have a wheat grinder, dehydrate plenty of corn for corn meal.

Melons - Pickle or dehydrate for a sweet treat.

Peppers - Dice and Freeze or dehydrate. The flavor and heat intensity will increase with freezing.

Cucumbers - Pickle

Cabbage - Ferment

Berries - Freeze, dehydrate, or can. These can best as jams, jellies or syrups.

Bananas - Dehydrate, or freeze in pre-measured amounts for recipes such as banana bread.

Squash - Many squashes cannot be canned due to their density. Freezing is best for most squash, and pumpkin is much easier to buy in a can at the supermarket.

Peaches - Can or Freeze

Apricots - Can or Freeze

Cherries - Can or freeze

Tomatoes - Can, freeze or dehydrate. Again, with tomatoes, you'll save time and frustration by buying already canned products at the supermarket. Skinning alone takes hours of time for large batches of tomatoes.

Apples - Can, freeze or dehydrate; can also be fermented for cider, although this takes up a lot of space.

Pears - Can, freeze or dehydrate.

Citrus - Can juice in ½ pint containers, and dehydrate zest.

Broccoli - Freeze or dehydrate.

Cauliflower - Freeze.

Beans (other than green beans) - Don't produce much when grown for the space they require, buy dry and prepare from that state, or can. Do not can refried beans.

Peas - Shell, then dehydrate or can.

Grapes - Freeze, dehydrate, or can as juice, jam or jelly. Can also be used for wine, which would be great for barter in a TEOTWAWKI situation.

Garlic - Dehydrate. Do not can or infuse in oil, as garlic is very susceptible to botulism.

The Baking Aisle – Most of the products we bake with are not far removed from their whole sources. Using whole-wheat flour takes practice and finesse. Begin experimenting with whole grains as you're building your stockpile, as whole-wheat flour tastes different, and bakes different, than store bought enriched white flour. An essential purchase for a TEOTWAWKI situation is a hand crank grain mill. This will allow you to grow or store whole grains and grind them into flour when you need them. Flours go rancid quicker than their whole grain counterparts, so it's better to store the whole grains than flour, especially if you're planning for a scenario where there is no power, or limited power, to keep things cool. Keeping things dry is also very important. You don't want those whole grains getting moldy. It can often be difficult to spot on whole grains, and ergot poisoning can have long-term catastrophic effects. Ergotism is believed to be the cause of the mass hysteria and physical symptoms that led to the Salem witch trials.

Sugar - Buy 25-pound bags, and re-package into gallon or quart zip type bags, double bagging for security. Pack those into a 5-gallon bucket with Diatomaceous Earth.

Flours - Buy 25-pound bags, and re-package into gallon or quart zip type bags, double bagging for security. Pack those into a 5-gallon bucket with Diatomaceous Earth. It's better, however, to buy and store whole grains, grinding either as you need them or for a week at a time.

Whole Grains - Buy 25 or 50 pound bags, and re-package into gallon or quart zip type bags, double bagging for security. Pack those into a 5-gallon bucket with Diatomaceous Earth.

Oils, lard, shortening - Buy shelf stable oils and solid fats that are long lasting and better for you. Stick with corn, olive, lard and coconut. Oils will go rancid, so store them in an environment that is as cool as possible, such as a root cellar or basement. Once the containers are opened, move them into a dryer area, and keep them as cool as possible.

Spices - Buy only what you can use in a year, as most herbs and spices will lose their flavor in that time, although they can safely sit on a shelf for five years. Even if on a small scale, plan for an herb garden and to grow basics like onions and garlic. It's amazing what some flavor will do for an appetite in a TEOTWAWKI situation.

Salt - Buy plenty, and keep it dry.

Baking powder - Buy plenty, and keep it dry. You'll be using this for bread rising once your yeast dies.

Yeast - Freeze for longer life.

Baking soda - Buy plenty, then buy some more. Baking soda has a myriad of uses besides baking, and you'll want plenty on hand. To keep dry, store in original packaging, then zip type bags, in 5 gallon buckets with diatomaceous earth.

Cornstarch - Like baking soda, buy plenty, then buy some more. Cornstarch is an excellent skin remedy for chafing and heat rash, and since you'll be doing more manual labor, it's excellent to keep on hand for those ailments.

Baking mixes - Baking mixes have some of the highest mark ups in the grocery business. Learning how to make your own saves you money, but is often time consuming. Also, the raw ingredients may not last as long as the baking mix when they are sitting on your shelf because your raw ingredients have no preservatives. While products with no preservatives are better for you in the long run, it shortens the amount of time you can safely store these products. If you're storing for a situation where your income would be reduced, find recipes online for your favorite baking mixes and use the money you'll save on other items. If you're stockpiling for a TEOTWAWKI situation, you'll want to make baking mixes a part of your preps.

Chocolate Chips and other silly baking additions - These are very necessary stock ups. Food fatigue is a very real issue in survival type situations, and our bodies may actually give us negative reactions such as nausea to a food we've been eating a lot of, which can be deadly in a survival type situation. Being able to add chocolate chips to pancakes or butterscotch chips to farina cereal can change the flavor of the food so that the body is less likely to reject it. So while these may be silly or non-essential items, you should have some on hand. They are also great for barter. Store them in the freezer while you can, and then the coolest environment you can find, double bagged, in 5 gallon buckets with diatomaceous earth.

The Dairy Aisle - Buying a cow is a great idea-in theory. In reality, a single cow takes at least eleven acres of quality grass to feed. If you don't have eleven acres, you're buying expensive hay, in addition to water, medications, and vet care for the cow. While it is a worthy investment if you have the space, make sure you do research on different breeds to determine which types are beneficial to your needs, and that you will have access to a bull during breeding season.

Milk - Buy powdered, and vanilla extract. It will never taste the same, but it will at least be drinkable with the addition of the vanilla. Powdered milk also works fine for baking and cooking, except for making pudding and gravy. Milk does freeze very well if you pour a cup or so out of the container prior to freezing, but it's impossible to store in large quantities.

Butter - Freeze, then keep as cool as possible. You may see information online regarding canning butter or ghee, but this cannot be safely done at home. You can buy commercially canned butter.

Margarine - Skip it if you can. Sticks freeze well, but you're better off buying butter, which will give better results when thawed. At half the price of butter it is a tempting addition to your stockpile, but it has no nutritional or long-term storage merit.

Eggs - Scramble, mix with a pinch of salt per egg, and freeze. Use ice cube trays for single eggs, small plastic containers for batches of three eggs for baking, and plastic zip type bags for large batches for cooking breakfast. Once the smaller measures are frozen solid, remove from containers and bag. While you may see information online regarding dehydrating eggs, it's not something that can be safely done at home. You can buy freeze-dried eggs online, which are much better for longer shelf life, but are rather expensive. Buying chickens is a viable option for many; an increasing number of municipalities are legalizing back yard chickens, making it possible for almost anyone to have fresh eggs. However, if you're planning on having chickens for the long term, you will need a rooster, and plenty of room for them to graze, unless you're also going to stockpile chicken feed. You'll also need space to allow them to brood, as established flocks will often peck chicks to death. Consider building chicken tractors to keep them somewhat free ranging but still protecting them from predators.

Sour cream - Does not store well, long term, in any form. You can buy powdered sour cream.

Buttermilk - The fats separate when frozen. You can buy frozen buttermilk, which works well for baking.

Cream cheese - It can be frozen, but loses the consistency for using raw. Works well in recipes that call for it to be fully cooked.

Cottage cheese - Does not store well, long term, in any form.

Hard cheeses - Hard cheeses freeze well, although frozen cheese is best cooked or melted rather than served raw. Grate, then freeze, as the cheese gets crumbly when frozen so it will not handle well if frozen in a block or in slices. American cheese does not freeze well. Velveeta, cheese whiz, and other types of processed cheeses are shelf stable for years.

Meats - Raising your own meat is a great goal, but something that requires good breeding stock, and a lot of land. In the long run, it may be cheaper to can or otherwise preserve your meat rather than trying to grow it, especially if you're living on a small homestead.

Chicken - Roast, strip the meat, then boil the carcass to make a broth. Can with the meat for bases for soups and stews; can without the meat for chicken broth to add to other recipes. You can buy canned chicken for use in recipes such as casseroles where you don't necessarily need the broth.

Beef Steak - Stick to cheaper cuts of steak like sirloin or round, and use for jerky. These steaks freeze well and often go on sale for reasonable prices.

Beef Stew Meat - With oxtail or other bones, make broth without any thickeners, and can for base for soups and stews. Only buy on sale, as meat sold as stew meat is often highly marked up.

Ground Beef - Cook as usual, with no seasoning, drain off all fat and rinse, then can. Buy the leanest ground beef you can find for long-term storage, because you need to have as little fat as possible in the product that you can. The more fat that is in a product, the quicker it will go rancid, even when properly canned. It is important that any meats you process in this manner are skimmed of as much fat as possible.

Beef Brisket or Roast - Cook in crockpot, can with resulting broth for base for meat and gravy meals, stroganoff, or soups. Brisket is normally priced at half the price of roast, and often goes on sale around Memorial Day. While not as tender as roast, it is a suitable substitute for many meals when slow cooked. This is not corned beef brisket, which can also be slow cooked and canned.

Pork Roast - Cook in crockpot, can with resulting broth for base for meat and gravy meals, or soups. Pork roast often goes on sale in early May and makes a rich, flavorful broth.

Pork Ribs - Cook in crockpot, can with resulting broth for base for meat and gravy meals, or soups like green chili. Ribs are higher in fat than many pork cuts and while they are often inexpensive cuts, they should not be your first choice for canning unless absolutely necessary.

Ham - Buy canned. Whole hams freeze well but modern smoking methods do not allow for preservation outside of freezing. Smoking is one of the least reliable ways of meat preservation.

Bacon - Freeze. Due to the high fat content, bacon is not suitable for canning.

Fish - Buy canned tuna, albacore and salmon. Salmon cans well but many other fish varieties end up very mushy when home canned. Freezes well.

Lamb - Freeze, or can.

Venison - Freeze, or can like beef. If you live rurally or even in the suburbs, hunting will be a great way to increase your protein consumption in a TEOTWAWKI scenario. It's a good idea to build a hoist mechanism that will hold enough weight for you to skin out an elk, if they are anywhere near your area. While you can have several days of fresh meat from a kill, you can, can the remainder over an open fire if need be, for long-term food preservation even while in the TEOTWAWKI scenario. This way none of your catch is going to waste.

Pork-based sausages - Freeze. Due to their high fat content, pork-based sausages are not suitable for canning. For long-term storage, grind your meat as for sausage, but without adding the fat. Can as you would ground beef. When serving, season with appropriate spices and serve as sausage gravy, crumbles in a casserole, or as Italian sausage in pasta sauce.

Staples

Rice - Buy in 25 or 50-pound bags, double bag in zip type bags, and store in 5 gallon buckets with diatomaceous earth. Also consider buying flavored rices to break up the monotony of your diet.

Coffee - Absolutely essential, both as a prep and as a barter item. Calculate how much you drink in a year, then purchase triple that. You'll have two years' worth of coffee and another year's worth to barter with.

Peanut Butter - Buy plenty, in 16 ounce jars.

Jelly - Buy or make plenty, in 16 ounce jars.

Honey - You cannot stockpile too much honey. It's a versatile sweetener, and works well to dress wounds.

Miscellaneous

Juices - These take up a lot of space in your stores, but can be a valuable source of needed liquids. If you have the room, stock enough for a gallon per week per four people.

Alcohol - In stressful situations, some people drink to help relieve stress. Alcohol can also be used to calm down someone who is upset, as a sedative, or to clean out a wound. You certainly don't want someone who is used to having a few drinks after work coming off alcohol cold turkey, either. Alcohol's most useful property, however, is as a barter tool. People will perceive it as a need. If you have it, you can use it to obtain something you need.

Soda - Absolutely skip stockpiling soda. It has no nutritional value. If someone in your family has a caffeine addiction, stockpile tea bags and work on switching them from soda to tea. Not only does it have less caffeine, making it a good way to taper down, it takes up far less room to stockpile.

Water - You will not stockpile enough water. If you live near a water source, buy a good filter and some good 50-gallon storage barrels. If you don't live near a water source, buy a good filter, more 50-gallon storage barrels to store rain and snow, and enough water in one-gallon containers for three months. The minimum standards for water storage are one gallon, per person, per day. If you have small children, or someone elderly, store three gallons for each of them, per day. You'll also need water for pets and livestock. Refill two and three liter soda bottles, but don't refill milk containers because it's nearly impossible to get all of the milk residue off the plastic, and that can contaminate your water supply. Save the milk containers for portable hot houses for your garden.

Paper goods - Don't neglect purchasing necessary paper goods for cooking. You'll need aluminum foil, plastic wrap, muffin tin liners, paper plates, bowls, cups, and plastic silverware. The less dishes you have to wash, the less water you will use.

Vitamins - Since you will be eating a calorie restricted diet, you will need to have a good stock of vitamins on hand to make sure you're getting your necessary nutrients.

Condiments - These are extras, but will help fight off food fatigue. Having mayo and pickles on the shelves is going to make those Vienna sausages much more palatable, because now they can be made into a sandwich instead of eaten straight out of the can.

Infant Formula - While "breast is best" takes on a whole new meaning in a TEOTWAWKI situation, as well as in a poverty type situation, sometimes things happen that require a change in plans. If someone who is of childbearing age is going to be with you for the long haul, it is a good idea to stock up on infant formula. If you end up not using the formula, it could become a valuable barter item. If you stockpile infant formula, make sure to donate it to a homeless shelter or food pantry at least two months before its expiration date, and get a receipt for the donation. The tax write off for the charitable contribution will help fund your restocking of this expensive prep item.

On buying processed foods - You're going to buy processed foods. Your preps are your business and no one is going to judge you because you have a case of canned ravioli or blue box macaroni and cheese in your pantry. If these are items you feel your family needs, then stockpile them. While ideally your preps are as natural and nutritious as possible, stockpiling familiar foods helps ward off food fatigue and makes it easier to take care of your family. It may also be essential to have quick meals available in the event that the head chef is busy tending livestock, in the garden, or dealing with an emergency. Just try to make sure that the bulk of your food preps, over time, are foods that are not heavily processed. There is a comfort in these foods for many people, but often the nutrition leaves much to be desired, and that's not something you want to skimp on, in a TEOTWAWKI scenario.

While food preservation is a great skill to learn, it takes practice to get it right, and time to build up a stock of home canned "convenience" food, or any type of food, to be truthful. Sometimes, canned processed food is a way to fill that gap to give your family a more balanced selection of food choices. Frankly, if TEOTWAWKI happened tomorrow, you would rather have a case of ravioli on hand than nothing. You should not feel bad because you have store brand canned tomato soup that you bought on sale rather than home canned tomato soup in pretty mason jars. You should feel a sense of accomplishment that you have provided a good meal starter for your family, no matter what the source. But as your stockpile grows, try to add foods with a higher nutritional value.

Conclusion

No matter what type of event you are prepping for, it's important to go about it in an organized way. Otherwise, you'll end up with a lot of bits and pieces of many meals, with nothing to really put together into something nutritious and edible-both very important facets of any meal, especially in either a poverty or TEOTWAWKI situation.

While there is something to be said for "hunger adds flavor," putting together a nutritious, yet edible meal insures that the people you're prepping for are both sated and fueled for what could be very hard manual labor. It's important that you find a good balance as you stockpile food.

Methods of food preservation are as unique as those that practice them. Not all of them will work for you and your family. It's perfectly all right if most of your stockpile is built from items you bought, on sale and with a coupon, at the supermarket, just as it's also perfectly okay if you love getting up before the sun to go milk your cow every day. You have to find what works best for your situation.

Canning is a valuable food preservation skill, and its importance not only for starting but for maintaining your food stockpile cannot be overlooked. If you learn how to can over an open fire or a wood stove, you can further preserve hunting bounty or shared food so that you will be able to get even more meals over time. Hunting isn't predictable, and in a TEOTWAWKI situation, close local game will exhaust itself in a suburban area. In a poverty situation, hunting is a great way to help fill the freezer as winter sets in, but the lack of predictability means that you could invest in a gun and a hunting license only to come home with no meat. But if you have the ability to can any hunting catch that is made, your food security lengthens over time and will continue to grow even if the likelihood of grocery stores reopening for business is minimal. Canning is such a valuable skill, in fact, that any preparation for TEOTWAWKI is not complete without its' mastery, because with no power, there will be no other way to insure a protein source over long cold winters without becoming migratory, like the animals you will be hunting.

Finally, even with the help of this guide, prepping or stockpiling food may seem a bit overwhelming to you especially at first. It's important to remember that everyone once started somewhere. Remember the tips that were mentioned in this guide.
- Set reasonable goals. It's great that you want to have one year's worth of food on hand. But it's better to plan for three days, then seven, then fourteen, and continue growing both your stockpile and your goal, than to try to coordinate the logistics of buying a year's worth of anything all at once.

- Start small. It's okay if, after your first week of shopping, you've only purchased enough supplies for one meal. You're working with what you can obtain. If it's October as you read this and you didn't have a garden this year, you're certainly going to have to have a major part of your stockpile come from the grocery store, for the first few months of your stockpiling adventure. Even with coupons and store sales, that can add up.

- Learn a new skill. If you can learn to can or dehydrate, you've just exponentially increased the amount of food you are able to stockpile for your family.

- Make your budget work for you. If you normally budget $30 a month for eating out, make home-made pizza or grab something from the dollar menu, and use the remainder of the money for prep items.

- If you get an income tax refund, use it to buy prep items like a good dehydrator, canning equipment, storage bags and buckets, etc. If you don't get an income tax refund, set aside $10 or $20 per week to buy these items.

- Make a plan, and stick to it. Your plan should reflect your goals, how you will obtain your food, your available skill set, your available tools, how you will preserve your food, and your budget.

Preparing for the future, no matter what your reason or what you're preparing for, does take hard work and diligence, but it doesn't have to be overwhelming or confusing! In time, the baby steps that you're taking now will turn into larger steps and you will begin to see real achievement. It brings a sense of accomplishment when you walk into your food storage area and realize that you have a month, or three months', worth of food on hand. As your preps continue to grow, you will find it easier to use what you have and fill in the gaps as things go on sale. Where before you could only buy one or two of a particular item that was on sale, at some point you'll be able to buy ten or twelve, because you will be paying full price less often.

While canning is the game changer in terms of long-term preps, growing your own food also greatly increases your chances for long-term food security. Whether you are prepping to avoid poverty cycles, or for an end of the world scenario, the skills, ability, space, and tools to grow your own food will substantially benefit your efforts. While it may be impossible to grow all of your own food in the city, there are many examples of people who have used the space they have in a creative manner, allowing them to grow more food than most people think is possible on city lots.

With the right mindset, prepping can be something that becomes a habit, rather than a hobby. If you are always in "prep mode," you will always be looking for ways to build your food stockpile in the most inexpensive ways possible. Once you've developed this mindset, it is much easier to plan for extremely long-term preps. Again, this is a mindset that will take months, if not years, to develop.

You should build your stockpile at your own pace, using your goals and your budget as a guide. Make the attempt to work towards zero waste and purchasing the healthiest foods that you can afford, for your family. Baby steps will guide your way in the beginning, but in time, you will find yourself making great strides to lead the lifestyle of your goals!

If you've enjoyed this book, please leave a review on Amazon and let us know your thoughts!

Discover more books:

Survival Kit Essentials: 10 Things to Keep You Alive

The Survivalist Cookbook - Recipes for Preppers

Prepping for Survival: 65 Supplies You Need to Live Through Anything

The Dead Road: Vol. 1 - Isolation

Bishop's Isle (Vol. 1)

Colony Z: The Complete Collection

www.ingramcontent.com/pod-product-compliance
Lightning Source LLC
Chambersburg PA
CBHW070837290526
45795CB00002B/890